P9-DEV-185

Amy Grant's

BY
AMY GRANT
WITH ROY AND DORIS NICHOLS
ILLUSTRATED BY JIM PADGETT

WORD PUBLISHING
Dallas • London • Vancouver • Melbourne

Thanks to Amy Grant's special friends for appearing with her on the cover.

Amy Grant's cover photo by Ben Pearson.

ISBN 0-8499-0710-1 (formerly ISBN 0-8344-0130-4)

Library of Congress Catalog Card Number 90-12327

Printed in the United States of America

94 95 96 97 98 99 LBM 10 9 8 7 6

PRESENTED TO Emma
BY

PREFACE

A story shared between parent and child is a precious time, especially when the story is a Bible story. This collection provides a rich resource of exciting Bible stories that will help children feel they are actually meeting the Bible characters and experiencing with them the events.

As you read, you'll notice that the stories are told in a language and with a perspective that can be understood by children. Often they are told from a character's point of view, perhaps as a child in the story might have told it himself. This approach helps a child identify with the story characters. It also helps him visualize a setting of real people in real places and separates the Bible story from the make-believe of fairy tales.

Careful attention is given to historical and geographical settings and to the details of everyday life in Bible times. The stories are retold as closely as possible to the biblical text within a child's understanding. In some cases events are "telescoped" to keep the stories within a child's attention span. Details that are inappropriate for children are omitted.

The stories in this collection have been chosen for their powerful spiritual principles which are as vital today as they were centuries ago. The questions following each story are designed to help parents and children share their feelings and experiences and apply the principles on a child's level.

May these ageless stories bring to life the greatness of God's love for his people, and may they plant a seed in each child's heart that will grow into a deep love for God and his word.

CONTENTS

Old Testament Stories

New Testament Stories

SIX WONDERFUL DAYS

No trees, no birds, no grass. There was not even any dirt where grass could grow. There was no sun to give light. It was before the beginning. Everything was empty and dark. But God was there.

So God made the light. He saw the darkness, and with the great power of his voice he said, "Let there be light." And the light began to shine where once there had been only darkness. Then God put the darkness in one place and the light in another. "Let's call the light day," he said, "and let's call the darkness night." Then God smiled and said, "This is good." That is what God did on the first day when he began making the world.

On the second day, God looked at the wet, shapeless world. The air was full of water and wet mist. Perhaps it was like a bad storm when the rain pours and the wind blows and there are big clouds. Then God spoke again, and the sky was there. God pulled the waters together. Some of the water he gathered into big, fluffy white clouds in the air. Some he left on the earth. This is what God made on the second day. God looked at his sky and said, "This is good."

On the third day God said, "Let there be dry ground." By the great power of God's voice, it happened. Big waves of water rolled to one side and to the other, and huge mountains came out of the water. Soon there were hills and valleys and flat ground. God gathered the waters

together and called them seas. The dry ground he called the land. God looked at what he had done and saw that it was good, but it needed something else. So God said, "Let plants grow on the land." And soon the ground was covered with all kinds of plants. There were flowers — big white daisies and yellow snapdragons — and vegetables like corn and peas and spinach. There were even trees with fruit already on them! This was the third day of God's creation. He had made many things this day.

Evening came, and then morning. It was the fourth day. But the world was not finished. God had made the sky, but it was empty. So God shaped a great yellow sun to give light and warmth to the earth in the daytime. He filled the night with the moon's soft light, and stars began to twinkle. God's world had become even more beautiful. The earth now had seasons — summer, winter, fall and spring. It also had days and years, and God had made them all. God looked at all that he had done on the fourth day. "It is good," he said.

The morning of the fifth day came, but God's work was not over. The sea and sky were too quiet. "Let's fill the waters

with sea animals," God said, "and let's fill the sky with birds." So the sea was filled with all kinds of living things. Some were so small you could hardly see them, and others, like the whales, were huge. Birds darted through the air and filled it with their singing. God liked what he had done so much that he told all the living things, "Have families so there will be many of you living in the sea and on the earth." God said, "They are good." Then evening came, and the fifth day of God's creation ended.

God looked at everything he had made. The sky was filled with birds, the seas were filled with fish, but the land was empty. So God said, "Let there be all kinds of animals." Soon the earth was covered with everything from great big elephants to tiny fuzzy caterpillars crawling on the leaves. God put stripes on the zebra, but polka dots on the leopard. He gave the centipede 100 legs and the snake no legs at all! God had filled the world with wonderful things.

First there was nothing — no trees, no birds, no grass — only God himself. Then, in five wonderful days, God in his love created our world.

But wait! What happened on the sixth day? Well, that's another story.

1. Why do you think God made the world?

2. What have you done to show someone you loved them?

GENESIS 1:26-2:24

A VERY SPECIAL DAY

It had been a busy day. Since early morning God had been at his work. It was now the sixth day of creation. Already, God had created a wonderful new world. It was filled with every kind of animal, both on the land and in the sea. Beautiful plants grew. Trees had fruit on their branches. Flowers bloomed, and birds flew overhead. They sang and made their nests in the trees that God had made. The sun shone brightly in the sky during the day. The moon and stars watched over the night sky. God had made it all, and it was good.

Now God was ready to do something very special. He would make man. This new creation would be different from the animals. In some ways, man would be like God. Man would be able to think. He would have a spirit, and God would love him and care for him in a special way.

So, on the sixth day of this new world, God took some dust from the ground and began to shape it. He gave the shape arms and legs. He made a head with eyes and ears, a mouth and a nose. He gave the shape a body. And then God breathed his own breath into the shape he had made, and it began to breathe and live. God had made a man. And he named this man Adam.

While God was making the earth, he had planted a special garden in a place called Eden. God had made this garden just for man. It had good soil for growing things. It had four rivers that brought cool, clear water into the garden. There was food to eat and beautiful trees to give shade and fruit. It was the perfect place for man. So God put Adam in the garden to watch over it and care for it.

Then God brought all the animals he had made to Adam. He showed them to Adam and said, "You must give names to each of these animals." What a big job that was! Adam carefully watched the animals to give each one just the right name. He gave names to all the animals God had made — the lion, the camel, the rhinoceros, the platypus and the hippopotamus. Then he gave names to the birds as well.

But something was missing. Adam needed someone to be with him and help him. Not one of these wonderful animals could share his thoughts. God knew just what to do. He made Adam go into a deep sleep. While he slept, God took a rib from Adam's side. Adam never even felt it. Carefully, God closed up Adam's side where the rib had been. Then God took that rib and made it into another shape. Again, God gave life to the shape he had made. It breathed and lived. God had made the first woman.

God took the woman and showed her to Adam. How happy Adam must have been. Now he would no longer be the only person in all of God's creation.

Adam said, "She will be called a woman because that means she was made from a part of me." Adam named her Eve. So, here in the garden that God had made for them, they became the first family in God's new world.

Now God had finished his creation, and he saw that it was good. When the seventh day came, God rested. His creation was finished. This ended the first week the world had ever known.

---

1. What is your favorite thing that God made? Why?

2. God made the Garden of Eden carefully so Adam and Eve would have a happy place in which to live. How do we help make our home a happy place to live today?

THE GREAT FLOOD

Noah and his three sons, Shem, Ham and Japheth, were farmers. They were good men who tried to get along with their neighbors. This was very hard because everyone else was always fighting and being cruel to each other.

One evening Noah rushed into his house, his eyes wide with amazement. Noah said, "A strange thing just happened! God spoke to me! He talked to me about all the evil that's in the world. He said he was going to put an end to it. Then he told me the strangest thing of all. He said, 'Make yourself a boat called an ark because I am going to flood the whole earth with water.' "

"How do you make an ark and how can we help?" asked Shem and Ham.

"When do we start?" asked Japheth.

"Right now," said Noah. "Here is God's plan for the ark. First, it has to be made of cypress wood. We are to make rooms in it and then cover it with pitch inside and out so that it won't leak."

"Dad, how big should we make it?" asked Shem.

"God told me that, too," said Noah. "It must be 450 feet long, 75 feet wide and 45 feet high."

"That's as high as eight men standing on each other's heads, and longer than our tallest trees!" said Ham. "Does it have to be so big just for us?"

"Yes, the ark must be a big boat. It will even have a lower, middle and upper deck. But it won't be just for us. We will take with us two of every kind of animal and bird — and seven of some!" said Noah.

Noah and his family had much to do. While they were building the boat, they were also gathering all the food they would need.

At last everything was ready. Two of every kind of animal and bird came to Noah to go into the ark. Then God said to Noah, "Take your wife, your sons and their wives and go into the ark. Also take the animals with you. After you're safe inside, I will make it rain for forty days and forty nights."

So Noah and his family and all the animals went inside. Then God shut the door to the ark. The rain poured from the sky, and water came up from the ground. The water rose higher and higher until it even covered the highest mountains. Everything on the earth died. Only those in the ark were safe.

After many days, the water started to go down. God sent a wind to help dry the earth. But it was still many months before even the mountains began to peek out above the water. Finally, the ark landed on the mountains of Ararat. Everyone was ready to be outside in the fresh air and to walk on the soft ground again, but it wasn't time to come out yet.

Noah waited inside forty more days and then sent out a dove. But it came right back because it couldn't find a dry place to land. Noah waited seven more days and sent it out again. That night it came back with a fresh olive leaf in its beak. Plants were growing on the earth again! Finally, after seven more days, Noah sent the dove out a third time. This time it did not come back. It had found a place to live on the earth!

After a few more days, God said to Noah, "Come out of the ark with your family and all the animals and birds."

Noah must have been very happy to get out of that boat. He gave thanks to God, and God was pleased. God promised, "Never again will I destroy everything with a flood. I've put the rainbow in the clouds to remind you of my promise." God had given everything a new beginning.

---

1. What do you think the world would be like if God had not told Noah to put the animals in the ark?

2. Noah and his family worked together to build the ark. What are some things you do in your family to work together?

GENESIS 13

FIRST CHOICE

Abraham stood on the rocky hill and looked down into the great green Jordan Valley to the east. The water sparkled in the sun as the river twisted and turned between the fields and vineyards. It was good to be at Bethel again. Abraham had built an altar and worshiped God here the last time he was in this land.

As Abraham looked out at the hills to the west, he could see his herders watching over the animals. The land was covered with cattle, sheep, donkeys and goats. Some of the animals belonged to Abraham and some to his nephew, Lot. Abraham had been faithful to God, and God had been especially good to Abraham and his family. The herds had grown larger and larger. Abraham and Lot had become very rich.

But Abraham was worried. He called to his servant. "Have you talked to the herdsmen today? Have there been any more quarrels between Lot's men and mine?"

"Yes, Master," the servant answered. "Every day there are more quarrels. There's not enough grass here for so many animals. That's why the men fight."

"I know you're right," Abraham said. "But Lot and I must not allow our herders to quarrel and fight. We're a family. I must think of something."

Abraham thought and thought. Bethel was a good place to live. He could tell Lot to take his animals and move away to other pastures. But what if Lot didn't want to take his flocks and herds to another place? What if he became angry ? Abraham loved his nephew and didn't want to quarrel with him. At last, Abraham went to talk with Lot.

"Lot, we must stop these arguments between your herders and mine. We're one family. There's enough land for both of us. Choose the part you want, and I'll take the other part. Then all our animals will have enough to eat."

Lot knew his uncle was being very kind. Since Abraham was older and head of the family, he should have first choice. But Abraham let Lot choose first. Lot looked to the east at the beautiful green land along the Jordan River. Then he looked to the dry hills and desert land to the west. He wanted the best land for himself.

"I'll take the land to the east," he told his uncle.

So Lot and Abraham divided their herds and said good-bye. Leaving Bethel and the green Jordan Valley behind, Abraham led his herds toward the dry hills to the west.

God was pleased when he saw how unselfish Abraham had been. "Abraham," God said, "look up from where you are standing. All the land to the north, to the south, to the east and to the west — all the land as far as you can see is yours. I give it to you. It will belong to you and your children and their children. You will have more children, grandchildren and great-grandchildren than you can count. Now, go. Travel across the land and see what I have given you."

Abraham was so happy. God had given him a new home and had promised to give him children of his own. Lot had taken the best land, but God had given Abraham the best blessing.

1. How did God reward Abraham for being unselfish?

2. What are some ways you can be unselfish with your family?

GENESIS 42-45:15

FAMILY REUNION

"What are we going to do, Father? There is no food or grain. All the animals are dying."

"I know, Ruben," Father replied. "This hot, dry weather has killed all the crops. But I've heard they have grain in Egypt. Go there and buy food for us and the animals, or we will die, too."

"May I go?" asked Benjamin, our youngest brother.

"No!" Father answered. "You must stay here with me. I don't want something to happen to you as it did to Joseph."

There it was again...the terrible lie I had told. I hadn't been there when my jealous brothers had sold our brother Joseph to the slave traders. But I had helped dip his coat in animal blood to make Father think an animal had killed him. I still felt guilty about what we had done. But there wasn't time to think about that now. We had a lot to do if we were leaving for Egypt tomorrow.

The next morning my nine brothers and I set out on our journey. Our donkeys carried empty grain sacks which we hoped to fill in Egypt. Soon we joined other travelers on their way to buy grain.

After many days of travel through hot, dry deserts, we reached Egypt. There we went to see the king's governor to buy grain. We kneeled before him touching our faces to the ground.

"Where is your home?" the governor asked.

"We live in Canaan. We have come to buy food."

"I think you have come to spy on us," he said.

I was frightened. How could he think such a thing? "Oh, no, great master. We have come here only to buy food. We live in Canaan with our father and younger brother who are at home. One of our brothers is dead."

"I will see if you are telling the truth, or if you are spies," he said. With that, we were locked in prison.

After three days the governor brought us out of the prison and said,"One of you must stay here in prison. The rest of you may take food back to your hungry family. But you must bring your youngest brother back to me to prove what you have said."

Then he pointed to my brother Simeon, and the guard took him off to prison. Next, our bags of grain were loaded onto our donkeys, and we started home.

When we reached Canaan again, we told our father all that had happened and what the governor of Egypt had said. He cried and cried. At first he would not let us go back to Egypt. But when there was no more food, he knew we must go back or we would die. Taking Benjamin, our youngest brother, we set out again.

As soon as we reached Egypt, we went to the governor. He treated us like guests. To our surprise, he seated us in order — from the youngest to the oldest. How did he know? Then he ordered a great feast, and Benjamin was given five times as much as the rest of us! After dinner our sacks were filled with grain.

Early the next morning we all left for home, happy to be together again. We had just reached the edge of the city, when a messenger stopped us.

"You have stolen the governor's silver cup," he said. We knew we hadn't stolen the cup. But when he searched us, he found the cup in Benjamin's bag! He took us back to the governor. We were so scared! How could we prove we hadn't stolen his cup?

The governor ordered everyone but us to leave the room. When he turned to look at us, he wasn't mad at all. His eyes were filled with tears. "I am Joseph, your brother," he said. "Tell me about my father."

None of us could speak. We had thought Joseph was dead. Would he punish us for sending him away years ago? But we did not need to be afraid.

"Don't blame yourselves for what you did," he said. "It was God who sent me here. Bring our father to Egypt so we can live together in this land." Then he threw his arms around us and cried with happiness. At last we were a family again.

1. What did Joseph do to show he loved his brothers?

2. How do you show your family you love them?

EXODUS 2:1-10

A Basket for My Brother

How excited I was. I had a new brother. Mother wrapped him in strips of soft cloth and placed him in my arms. His fingers were so tiny. "I can hardly wait to show him to my friends," I said.

"Miriam!" My father's voice was stern. "You know what will happen if the Egyptians find out we have a baby boy in this house. They will take him and kill him! We must keep him hidden. When he cries, you must quiet him quickly. No one must know he's here."

At first it was easy . His small voice could not be heard outside the house. Much of the time he slept. But as days passed, his voice grew stronger, and he stayed awake more. Finally one day Mother said, "Miriam, we can't hide your brother any longer. He's getting too big. Your father and I have a plan, but you must help."

As Mother explained the plan to me, Father cut armloads of reeds that grew along the riverbank. From them Mother wove a small basket and covered it inside and out with tar and pitch so it wouldn't leak. It was like a little boat, just large enough to hold my brother. Gently Mother placed him inside.

We walked down the Nile River to the spot where the Egyptian princess always came to bathe. There Mother set the basket in the river. I hid and waited. Soon I heard the laughing voices of the princess and her servants as they came down the path. Just as they got to the edge of the river, my little brother began to cry. The princess stopped.

"What's that in the water? Get it for me," she said to one of her servants. The girl waded into the water and picked up the basket. Now my brother was really crying. The princess peeked inside.

"Look, it's one of the Hebrew babies," she said. Gently she picked up my brother and held him close to quiet him.

I ran from my hiding place and bowed before the princess. "Would you like for me to get one of the Hebrew women to take care of the baby for you?" I asked.

"Yes," she said. "Go and get one."

I ran as fast as I could to Mother who was waiting for me. "He's safe. Come quickly," I said, taking her by the hand.

Mother and I hurried back to the princess who was holding the baby in her arms. The princess said to Mother, "Take this baby and care for him. I'll pay you for your work."

Mother was so happy. Our plan had worked. My brother, whom the princess would later name Moses, was safe, and we could care for him and watch him grow. God had taken care of our family.

1. Who helped Miriam and her parents save baby Moses?

2. Miriam obeyed her mother and father. What do you do to obey your parents?

JOURNEY TO FREEDOM

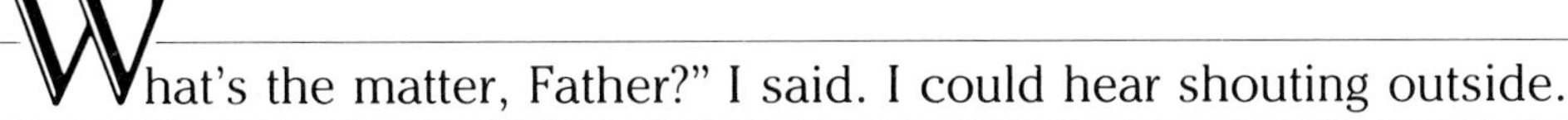

"What's the matter, Father?" I said. I could hear shouting outside.

"The Pharaoh himself has ordered us to leave Egypt. We must hurry!"

Could it be true? Were we really leaving at last? Our people had been slaves in Egypt for 400 years. Would we finally be free?

Noise filled the air as people hurried to load their belongings on the backs of animals or into carts. Thousands of sheep and other animals were being herded together. As the news spread, more and more people came. It seemed as if all of Egypt were going with us.

Finally the long lines began to move. Little by little we left the city of Rameses behind. I wondered what it would be like in this new land God had promised to us. What would it be like to be free without a slave master telling you what to do?

At first it was exciting and fun, but I was getting tired by the time we reached the edge of the desert. I wanted to rest. Then a strange thing happened. A great cloud appeared in front of us. All day it moved just ahead of us. At night the cloud became a tower of fire. It gave enough light so we could even travel in the dark.

"The Lord is leading us out of Egypt," Father explained.

Finally, we came to a sea. Behind us was the desert. Ahead was only water. What would we do now? Some of the people began to complain. Others were afraid. None of us would feel safe until we were far away from Pharaoh and his army.

"How will we get across the sea?" I asked.

"We must trust God. He will tell Moses what to do," Father replied.

Suddenly people began to shout and point to a cloud of dust over the desert where we had just been. "It's the Egyptians! They've come to take us back!"

Hundreds of soldiers riding on horses and in chariots were racing across the desert to get us. I was scared. People began to shout and cry, "We'll all be killed! Why did we let Moses bring us out here to die?"

Then we heard the voice of Moses. "Don't be afraid. Stand still where you are. The Lord will fight your battle for you if you will be quiet."

"Look! The great cloud is moving," a scout shouted.

It was no longer going ahead of us. It moved between us and the Egyptians. On their side of the cloud it was dark. On our side it was light. All night the cloud protected us from the Egyptians.

Then Moses stood before the sea. He held his hand over the water, and a great wind began to blow. The water piled up in great waves as the wind pushed it back and divided it. Like a long hallway, the water stood up on the left and the right. Between the walls of water the wind turned the mud to dry ground. God had made a way for us to cross the sea. Quickly all the people and animals began crossing on the dry land.

In the morning light, the Egyptians saw what was happening. "After them!" they shouted. The Egyptian chariots began to follow us into the path across the sea. For a moment it seemed the terrible war chariots would run over us. Then the chariots began to turn and twist out of control. The soldiers couldn't seem to drive the horses.

"Let's get out of here and away from these Israelites," they said. "Their God is fighting for them and against Egypt."

As they tried to turn and go back, Moses stretched his hand over the sea again. Behind us, the walls of water tumbled in on the Egyptians. The sea rolled back over Pharaoh's army. Soon all was quiet. No Egyptians were left, but all our people were safe on the other side of the sea. God had saved us. We were free!

1. When the people were afraid of the Egyptian army, how did God help them?

2. Tell about a time when you were frightened. Who helped you to have courage?

JOSHUA 2

SPIES ON THE ROOF

"I have an important job for you two, but it will be dangerous," said Joshua, the new leader of Israel. "The Lord has spoken to me. It's time for us to cross the Jordan River and take the land God has given us. I want you to go secretly into Jericho. You must find out all you can about the city and the land around it."

My friend and I were excited. Spies! We were going to be spies for God. It was scary, but God would protect us.

It was late afternoon by the time we crossed the Jordan River and reached the city of Jericho. It had a thick wall around it. This wasn't going to be easy!

Many people were hurrying into the city. We hoped we would not be noticed in the crowd. Keeping away from busy streets, we explored the strange city. Cold shivers ran up my back. I was afraid that at any minute the king's soldiers might find us.

"We must find a place to stay for the night," my friend said. "It's getting late."

"Look, there's a house built on the wall. It has a back window where we could get outside the city walls without being seen. Let's see if we can get a room there."

Rahab, the owner of the house, welcomed us. When we were inside, she said, "You are Israelites! Are you the spies the king is looking for?"

My friend and I were terrified. Had we walked into a trap?

Suddenly there was shouting in the street below. Soldiers were running toward the house.

"Quick!" Rahab said. "Go up onto the roof. You can hide under the flax plants drying there." We ran up on the roof, and Rahab covered us with the plants. We lay as still as possible, listening as she hurried back into the house.

"Rahab! Open up in the name of the king!" the soldiers shouted as they banged on the door.

"What do you want?" she asked.

"Two men came here earlier. We think they're Israelite spies."

"Yes," she said calmly. "Two men did come here just before dark, but they left the city."

We held our breath and waited. Would the soldiers believe her? Would they search for us? Would they look on the roof?

"I have no idea which way they went," said Rahab. "You must hurry and catch them before they can get away." We heard the soldiers rush outside and close the city gate behind them. When it was safe, Rahab came and uncovered us.

"Why have you done this?" I asked as we crawled from our hiding place.

"I know your God has given this land to you," she said. "Everyone has heard how your God helps you win over your enemies. Your God is the God of heaven. That's why I helped you. Now promise you will save my family and me when you capture Jericho."

"You have helped us, so we will help you," we said. "Leave a red cord hanging in your window. And be sure you and all your family are inside this house when we attack Jericho. Then you will not be harmed."

Rahab let down a long rope from the window over the wall so we could escape. God had used Rahab to protect us. With the Lord's help we would protect her when we returned to capture Jericho.

---

1. Why was Rahab kind to the spies?

2. How do we show kindness to others in our homes?

A Sound of Trumpets

What an exciting time to be in Jericho! Three days ago my sister Rahab had helped the spies from Israel. We knew that the Israelites would soon capture our city, but we believed the spies' promise that we would be safe. My whole family had moved into Rahab's house as they told us to do. The red rope the spies had used to escape still hung in the window over the wall.

For three days I had watched the camp of Israel across the Jordan River, but nothing had happened. On the fourth morning, Rahab called out, "Look! The Israelites are breaking camp." Sure enough, their leader, Joshua, was lining them up.

"Look at the river!" I shouted. "The water is piling up. The river isn't flowing anymore. And there's a dry path across the river where the water used to be!"

We watched the priests carry the holy ark to the middle of the Jordan and stop. With God's help all the people crossed the river on dry ground.

A guard standing on the wall around the city shouted, "The Israelites are coming! Sound the alarm!"

Suddenly Jericho was in total confusion. The great city gates were closed and barred. Soldiers ran to their stations on the walls. Surely the Israelites would soon attack the city.

But nothing happened. The Israelites camped on the plains outside the city. Days passed. Jericho was tightly locked so no one could come in or leave. Everyone was just waiting in fear.

Finally, one day we heard the sound of trumpets. I looked out the window, expecting to see all the soldiers of Israel. But there was no army. There was just a small group of soldiers, followed by seven priests carrying trumpets. Behind them were more priests carrying the ark of the Lord. Following them was another group of soldiers. We could hear the trumpets, but no one said a word. Joshua gave an order, and they began marching all the way around the city without saying a word. Then they just went back to their camp.

The next day the same thing happened — and the next day and the next — for six days. The people of Jericho began to wonder, "What are they doing? Why doesn't Israel attack?"

At daybreak on the seventh day the Israelites started marching again, just as before. But this time they kept on marching. Again and again they marched around the city. They marched until they had gone around the city seven times. Then they stopped. Everything was very quiet. Suddenly the priests blew the trumpets, and all the people gave a mighty shout!

The house began to shake. There was a rumbling noise, and then a roar. I could hardly believe my eyes. The great, thick, tall walls of Jericho were crumbling. Soon only a cloud of dust was left where once the great walls had stood. God had torn down the walls of Jericho. With a mighty rush, the soldiers of Israel ran into the city.

I was so scared. Would the two Israelites remember their promise to save us? A banging on the door made me jump. As Rahab opened it, I saw the two men we had hidden on the roof. They had kept their promise.

"Come quickly," they said. "We must get out of the city!"

They hurried us through the streets and over the fallen walls to the camp of the Israelites. Flames from the burning city lit the sky, and great clouds of smoke climbed into the air. Ashes sprinkled down on us. The king's palace and the temple of the false god Baal crashed to the ground. Jericho was gone.

The spies had kept their promise, and God had kept his. We had all seen the wonderful power of God. And he had kept us safe.

---

1. What did God do to help Israel capture Jericho?

2. The spies kept their promise to Rahab. Why is it important for us to keep the promises we make?

LET ME GO WITH YOU

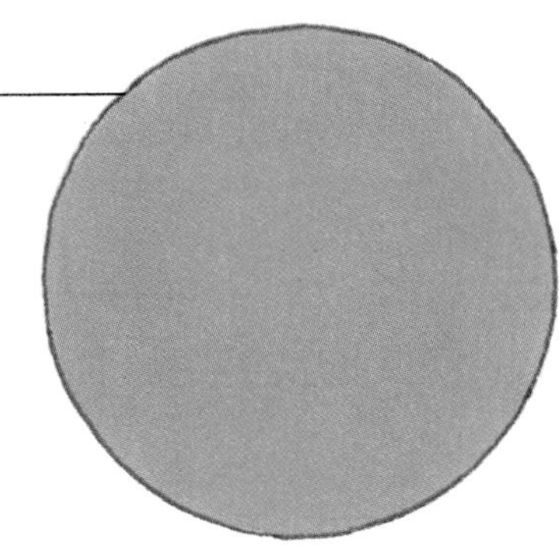

Naomi wiped her eyes. This was a sad time in her life. But crying would not change matters, and she must decide what to do. Her husband had died long ago, and now her two sons were dead also. Only she and her sons' wives, Ruth and Orpah, were left.

"I have decided to go back to my homeland of Judah," Naomi said. "I have relatives there, and I am too old to start a new life here in Moab. You two must go back to your own families as well."

Sadly, Orpah agreed and returned to her home, but Ruth would not leave Naomi. She loved her dearly. "Please do not ask me to go away from you," she said. "Wherever you go I am going. I will serve your God. I will learn to love your people, and I will stay with you until I die."

Naomi saw that Ruth would not change her mind. So they packed their things and traveled to Bethlehem in Judah. They arrived at a busy time of the year. The barley was ripe in every field. The grain harvest was about to start.

The two women moved into Naomi's small house. "How are we going to get food?" asked Ruth. "We have nothing to live on."

"Israel has a law to help the poor," said Naomi. "Any stalks of grain dropped by harvesters must be left on the ground. They must also leave grain around the edges of the fields. The poor people are allowed to follow behind the workers to pick up that grain for themselves."

"Then I will gather the grain in the barley fields for us," said Ruth.

"I wish you didn't have to do such hard work, Ruth, but there is no one else to feed us," Naomi said.

So, early the next day Ruth went into the field of Boaz, a rich farmer. One by one she picked up the few stalks of barley that had been left behind. How hard she worked. Her back was tired from bending over so much, but still she followed the workers in the hot sun.

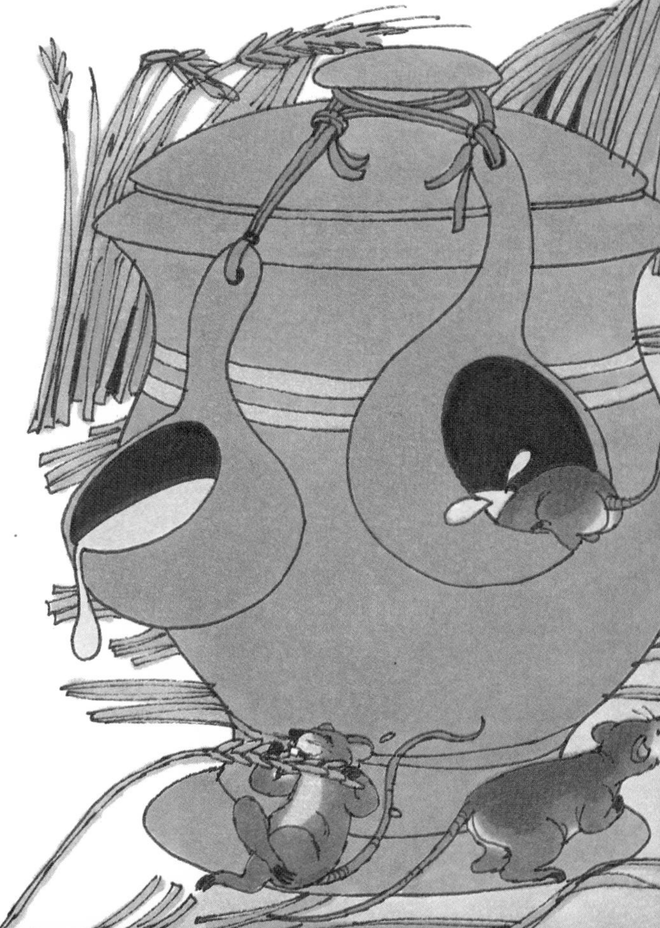

"Who is that young woman?" Boaz asked one of his men.

"She is Ruth who came back from Moab with Naomi. She has worked hard all day."

Boaz's heart went out to Ruth, and he said, "Stay here in my field. No one will harm you. You may drink water from my jars when you are thirsty."

"I am a stranger in this country. Why are you being kind to me?" Ruth asked.

"I have heard how kind you are to Naomi. May the God of Israel reward you for your goodness," Boaz answered.

Then Boaz gave Ruth some food, and he told his men to leave extra grain behind for her. All through the harvest Ruth worked hard so she and Naomi would have food. Boaz watched her and made sure no one troubled her.

When the harvest ended, the farmers began to thrash the barley. They dragged flat sleds over it to separate the grain from the stalks. Women tossed the grain into the air so the wind would blow away the straw. After the hard work was over, a festival was held.

Late that night Boaz noticed Ruth nearby. She wanted to be his wife, and he agreed. Ruth went home with a gift of grain for Naomi from Boaz. He went to the town leaders and made arrangements for their wedding.

So Ruth and Boaz were married. God blessed their home and gave them a baby. They named him Obed. Naomi was proud of her new grandson. She had a right to be proud because Obed would grow up to become the grandfather of a famous king of Israel.

1. How did Ruth show her love for Naomi?

2. What can you do to help take care of people in your family?

GIVEN TO GOD

Hannah had made her yearly trip to the Lord's house with her husband to worship God. But she was very unhappy. "I wish I had a son. All of the wives I know have children but me. I am so sad I don't even want to eat." As she prayed, she cried and made a promise to the Lord. "Oh great God, if you will let me have a son, I will give him back to you. He will serve you all his life."

Now Eli, the high priest, was standing nearby watching as Hannah prayed. He wondered what had made this kind woman so sad. Hannah told Eli how she had been praying to the Lord to give her a son.

"Go then, and may the God of Israel answer your prayers," Eli said.

So Hannah left the Lord's house, and she was no longer sad.

God remembered Hannah and her prayers. He blessed her and her husband Elkanah with a son. Hannah was so happy! She named the child Samuel because that means "asked of God."

When Samuel was almost three years old, he and his parents made another trip to the Lord's house at Shiloh. After they had worshiped, they went to see Eli. "Do you remember me?" Hannah asked. "I am the woman you heard praying to God for this child. God answered my prayer and gave me what I asked. Now I am giving my son to the Lord as I promised." It was very hard for Hannah to leave the son she had wanted so badly. But she had promised to give him to God. So Elkanah and his family returned to their home in Ramah, but Samuel stayed with Eli and served in God's house.

Every year Samuel's parents visited him when they came to worship. His mother always brought him a fine robe that she had made to go with the long linen shirt he wore in the Lord's house. They loved Samuel so much.

God loved Samuel, too, and the boy pleased God with his service. In fact, he was liked by everyone who knew him.

One night a most unusual thing happened. While Samuel was sleeping, he heard someone call his name. Thinking it was Eli, he got up, went to the priest and asked, "Did you call me?"

"I didn't say anything," Eli answered. "Go back to sleep."

Samuel was puzzled. He was sure someone had called him. But he went back to bed as Eli had told him.

Later, Samuel heard someone call his name again. He got back up and hurried into Eli's room the second time. "Here I am. You called me?" Samuel said.

Now Eli was puzzled. He hadn't called for Samuel. "I didn't call," Eli said. "Go back to bed and go to sleep." So Samuel went back to bed.

"Samuel. Samuel!" There it was again. Someone was calling him. So Samuel got up and went to Eli the third time. "Here I am. You called me."

This time Eli understood. It was God speaking to Samuel. "Go lie down," Eli said. "If he calls you again, say, 'Yes, Lord, I hear you.'"

Samuel did as he was told and went back to bed. Soon the Lord came and stood beside him. He said, "Samuel! Samuel!"

"Yes, Lord, I hear you," Samuel answered.

Even though Samuel was just a boy, God gave him an important message for Eli. This wasn't the only time God spoke to Samuel. As Samuel grew, the Lord continued to be with him. Everyone in Israel knew that Samuel was a prophet of God.

1. How can you tell that Samuel's family loved him very much?

2. Samuel served God all his life, even when he was a child. What are some things you and your family can do to serve God?

1 SAMUEL 17:1-52

A GIANT FOR THE KING

It isn't easy being the youngest in the family, especially when you have seven brothers. I've always been "Little David." Well, I'm a teenager now, and I can do important things too. That's why my father sent me to take grain and bread to my three brothers. They were fighting in a war against the Philistines.

When I got to the camp, I heard yelling and shouting. Soldiers were running everywhere. To see what was happening, I climbed over some rocks and looked into the valley below. I could hardly believe it. There in a field stood a mean-looking giant. He was huge. A great bronze helmet covered his head, and he wore shiny metal armor. Even his legs were covered. He had a long pointed stick hanging over his back and a huge spear in his powerful hands. There he stood, making fun of the army of God.

"Why don't you send someone out to fight me," he yelled. "If he can kill me, the Philistines will be your servants. If I win, then Israel will be our slaves. I, Goliath, challenge you!"

"Who's going to fight him?" I asked the commander.

"King Saul has offered a great reward to anyone who will fight the giant, but no one has tried," he replied.

"I'll fight him!" I said, and in a few moments I was surprised to find myself talking with the king.

"But you're just a boy. Goliath has been a soldier all his life," said the king.

"I may be young, but I can fight," I answered. "Once while I was watching over our sheep, I killed a bear and a lion that tried to get the lambs. The Lord protected me then, and I know he will protect me from that ugly Philistine too."

"Then you must wear my armor," said the king. However, King Saul was a very big man. I could hardly lift his long heavy sword, and his armor swallowed me. The helmet covered my face; I couldn't even see where I was going!

"I can't wear all this. I don't know how to use such things," I said. I didn't need a king's armor. I already had a plan.

My hands were shaking a little as I picked up my shepherd's stick and my slingshot. I walked down to the stream where I picked up five smooth stones and put them in my bag. At close range Goliath looked even larger than before. I knew I had to be brave and ask God to help me.

When Goliath saw me, he began to yell, "What's this? You're just a kid!" He looked at my shepherd's stick. "Do you think I'm some dog you're going to beat with a stick?"

"You've come out to fight me with your spear and sword," I said. "But I've come to fight you in the name of God. He will help me win. Then all the world will know about the God of Israel."

Angrily, Goliath began moving toward me. I took one of the stones from my bag, put it in the sling and whirled it over my head. The stone whooshed through the air. There was a thud; the stone had struck Goliath's forehead. He crashed to the ground! I ran over to him, grabbed his own sword and killed him. When the Philistines saw he was dead, they turned and ran. Israel was safe again.

God had protected me. He had used me, a young boy with just a stone and a slingshot, to defeat a giant. But with God on my side, that was all I needed!

---

1. What had David learned to do as a shepherd that helped him win over Goliath?

2. David trusted God and used what he had learned to serve God. What things are you learning to do at home that you might use to serve God?

THE WIDOW'S JAR

The prophet Elijah was tired. He had walked mile after mile as the hot sun burned down upon him. As he reached the top of a small hill, he could see the town of Zarephath in the distance. Near the town gate a woman and her son were picking up sticks.

"Why are you so sad, Mother?" the boy asked.

"There is no food in our house, my son. We have only a handful of flour and a little oil. When that is gone, we will have nothing left to eat."

"Look, Mother. Someone is coming," the boy said. "Why is he dressed like that —with leather around his waist and an animal skin over his shoulders?"

"He looks like one of the prophets from Israel," she said. "He will wish he had not come here. It's been so long since it has rained. No plants are growing. There is no food in Zarephath. Come, help me gather up a few twigs so we can go home and cook our last bit of food."

Elijah stopped and called to them, "Could I have a little water to drink?"

He looked so tired and thirsty. His worn sandals showed that he had walked a long way.

"Yes, I will bring you some water," the mother answered.

"Could I have a piece of bread, too?" Elijah asked.

The boy looked at his mother and then at the hungry man. There was no bread in the house. What would she do?

"I have no bread," she told him. "I have only a handful of flour in my flour jar. There

is just a small bit of oil left in the oil jug. I will use these sticks to build a fire and cook some bread for us to eat. Then there will be nothing left to keep us alive."

"Don't worry," Elijah said. "Go to your house and do what you planned. But first make me some bread from your flour and oil and bring it to me. Then, make some for you and your son."

The woman looked at Elijah. Should she share her last bit of food with this tired, hungry man?

As if reading what was in her mind, Elijah said, "The Lord God of Israel has told me that the flour in your jar will not run out, and the jug of oil will not be empty."

The woman looked at Elijah for a moment. Then she turned and walked back to her small stone house. There she built a fire and set a flat griddle over it to heat. Taking the last handful of flour from the jar, she mixed it with water. Then she patted out a small flat circle of dough and poured the last few drops of oil on the hot griddle. It sizzled as the dough began to cook. Soon the delicious smell of frying bread filled the air. When the bread was cooked, she took it from the griddle and gave it to Elijah.

"Now, make some bread for you and your son," he said.

Slowly, she reached again into the flour jar. "There is as much flour now as there was before I made your bread," she said excitedly. Quickly she picked up the oil jug and shook it. "And there is as much oil as before!"

It was just as Elijah had said. Neither the oil jug nor the flour jar would be empty until the Lord sent rain again so that the land would have food. The widow had done as the prophet had asked. She had believed God and his prophet Elijah. And God had given her all the food she needed because she had shared with others.

---

1. God wants us to trust him. When did God begin to refill the jugs of flour and oil?

2. The widow was a kind woman who shared even her last meal. How do we show kindness to others?

2 KINGS 4:8-37

A Special Gift

I am Gehazi, servant of Elisha the prophet of God. Sometimes I think my master can do anything. Wherever we go, he uses the gifts God has given him to do good.

We often go through the city of Shunam on our way to northern Israel. We like to spend the night there. Many times when Elisha and I are traveling, we have to sleep on the ground under a tree with only our coats for cover. But we have friends in Shunam. A woman and her husband built a small room on their house just for us. It has a bed, a table and a chair. A lamp gives us light at night.

On one of our visits, Elisha said to the woman, "You have done many kind things for us. Is there something we can do to show our thanks?"

"I don't need anything," she said. "I have a good home here with my friends and family."

"There is one thing she does not have," I told Elisha. "She has no son, and her husband is getting old. A son would make her very happy, and he could take care of her when he grows up."

Elisha liked my idea. He called the woman to him and said, "About a year from now, you will have a son."

She could not believe what she had heard. But just as Elisha had promised, a baby boy was born to them. As he grew up, he learned to help his father.

One hot day as they were working in the field, the boy suddenly felt a terrible pain in his head. "My head, my head," he cried out.

"Quickly! Take the child to his mother," the father ordered.

All through the morning she held him on her lap, but it was no use. About noon the child died. Sadly, the mother carried him to Elisha's room, laid him down, shut the door and went outside. She called to her husband, "Please send me a servant with a donkey. I am going to find Elisha the prophet."

While this was happening, Elisha and I were at Mount Carmel, twenty miles away. That is a long way to ride a donkey, but the woman said to her servant, "Go as fast as you can. Don't slow down unless I tell you."

When she reached us, she fell to the ground, crying. Elisha understood. "Something is wrong with the boy," he said.

"Hurry, Gehazi. Run as fast as you can to the boy. Don't stop or speak to anyone."

I did as Elisha had said and began the long run back to Shunam. Elisha and the boy's mother came behind me as quickly as they could. I reached the house first, but I couldn't help the boy.

When Elisha got there, he went into the room where the boy was, closed the door and began to pray. He laid down over the boy and put his face against the boy's face. He covered the boy's hands with his own. Slowly, the child's body began to warm. Elisha got up. Back and forth he paced. Then once again, he spread himself over the boy as he had done before.

Suddenly, I heard a sneeze, then another and another. The boy sneezed seven times, and then he opened his eyes. He was awake. He was alive!

"Call the boy's mother," Elisha said.

She couldn't believe it. Because she had been kind to Elisha, God had now given her the same wonderful gift twice — the life of her son.

---

1. Why did Elisha want to do something special for the woman from Shunam?

2. The Shunamite woman's son was very special to her. What are some things that make you special to your family? What things make your family special to you?

DANIEL 6

LIONS IN THE NIGHT

Daniel was a young Hebrew who had been captured and taken to Babylon, a foreign country. Even though Daniel lived in Babylon, he never forgot to worship the God of Israel. He always did his best and was honest and truthful. Three times each day he bowed down and prayed to God. God blessed Daniel, and he became an important ruler in the kingdom.

One day King Darius noticed Daniel and said, "What a good worker. I'll put Daniel in charge of all the other officers in my kingdom."

When the other officers heard this, they were very jealous. "We must find something bad to tell the king about Daniel. Then he won't get the new job."

But no matter how hard they tried, they couldn't find anything bad to tell the king. Daniel didn't steal from the king's treasury, he didn't lie when he made reports, and he always did his job well.

But Daniel's enemies didn't give up. They thought of a plan. One morning they came to Darius and said, "O great king, we think you should make a new law. For the next thirty days, if any person bows down and prays to anyone except you, throw him into a den full of lions."

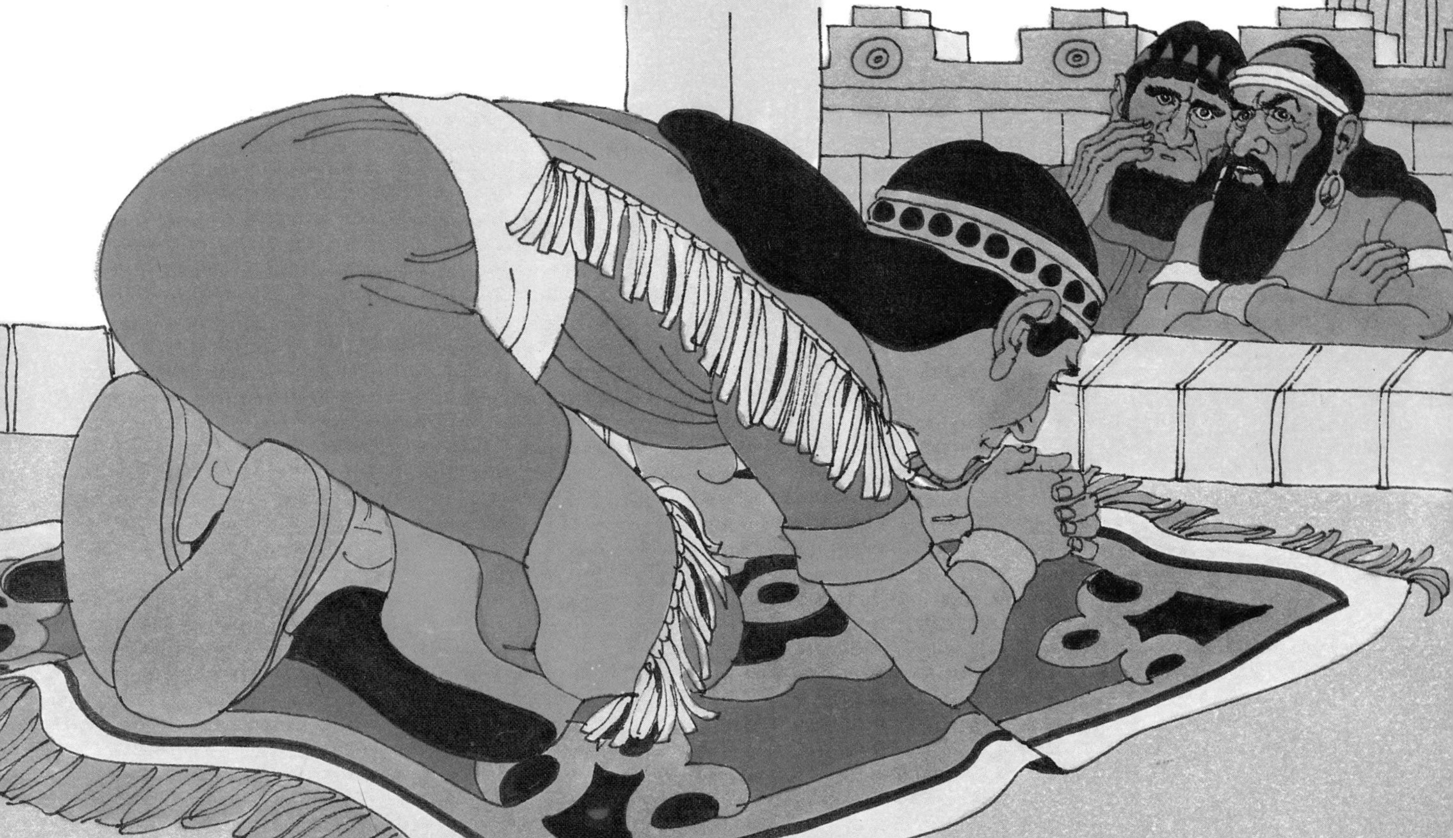

Perhaps the king thought the men were honoring him. Perhaps he thought he would enjoy seeing people bow down and pray to him. Certainly he did not think about Daniel who prayed only to God. So the king wrote the law, signed it and sent it to all the kingdom. After a law was written and signed, not even the king could change it.

The men who had tricked Darius watched to see what Daniel would do. Would he stop praying to God, or would he break the law?

When it was time to pray, Daniel went upstairs and opened a window facing Jerusalem, his old home. Then he fell to his knees and prayed, giving thanks and asking for God's help.

Daniel had broken the new law. The evil men could hardly wait to tell the king! "Remember the law you made which said that everyone must pray to you or be thrown into the den of lions?"

"Yes," said the king. "That is the law, and it cannot be changed."

"Well, that man Daniel pays no attention to you or your laws. He prays to his God three times each day."

The king had been tricked. What could he do to save Daniel? All day he thought, but no matter how much he wished, there was nothing he could do.

Sadly, he called for Daniel to be

brought to him. "I pray that your God will save you from this," he said.

So Daniel was put in with the ferocious lions, and a stone was rolled over the entrance. The king's own seal was put on the door so no one could open it.

All night long the king stayed awake. He was so sad and worried about Daniel that he couldn't eat or sleep. When the first light of morning came, the king hurried to the lions' den. As he came near, he shouted, "Daniel, has your God saved you from the lions?"

"I'm safe, great king," Daniel answered. "The lions haven't hurt me because God sent an angel to close their mouths. I have done nothing wrong to you so God has taken care of me."

The king was so happy. He could hardly believe Daniel was really alive. When Daniel was taken from the den, he didn't have one scratch on him. God had kept him safe. So the king made a new law telling all the people everywhere to honor and fear the God of Daniel.

1. What did Daniel do that caused him to be put into the lions' den?

2. Sometimes it is hard to do what is right when others do not. How can we help each other do our best and make good choices?

A Night to Remember

At last I am old enough to stay with the other shepherds in the fields and on the hillsides while the sheep graze. We will camp out here with the sheep as long as there is enough grass for them to eat. Each night we bring the flocks into the stone and brier pen for protection. During the night we take turns watching for wolves and other wild animals. When we are not on watch, we roll up in our camel hair coats in front of the door to the sheep pen. It is our job to protect the sheep.

Late evening is a special time for shepherds. We gather around the campfire and share the adventures of the day. Sometimes the older shepherds tell stories of long ago. My favorite story is about David, the shepherd who killed a lion and a bear to protect his sheep. He was just a boy like me, but he grew up to be one of the great kings of Israel.

This night began like many others, but it was to be a very special night. I was leaning on my staff, watching the fire and listening to stories. Suddenly, a great light shone around us. Everyone stopped talking. A strange form came out of the darkness. It was an angel! We trembled and moved back in fear.

Then a voice said, "Don't be afraid. I bring you good news. It is a message of great joy for all people everywhere. This day Christ the Lord, your Savior, has been born in Bethlehem. This is how you will know him. He is a baby wrapped in strips of cloth. He is lying in a manger."

Then the sky was filled with angels. They began singing beautiful words of praise, saying, "Glory to God in the highest. Peace on earth. Good will to men."

With that the angels disappeared into the night sky. For a moment no one spoke. Then everyone began to talk at once. "What does this mean?" one asked.

"It is the promised Savior," cried another. "He is the one the prophets told us about!"

"Yes," said another. "This is a message from the Lord. Let's go to Bethlehem to find the baby."

We hurried through the night, climbing up the hillside toward Bethlehem. As we reached the edge of town, we could see the camps of many people. Some were sleeping in the caves in the hillsides where animals are usually kept.

"Why are there so many people here?" I asked an old shepherd.

"Haven't you heard? It's tax time. The Roman ruler has ordered each family to go back to the father's birthplace to be taxed. All these people have returned here to pay the Roman tax. Every guest house is full. That's why all these people are camping out like shepherds or are sleeping in the stables."

The crunch of our footsteps on the rocky path broke the silence as we hurried through the town. Then we saw it. Ahead in one of the stable caves there was light and movement. Could this really be the place? Would the Lord send the Savior to be born here among the poor people of Bethlehem...to be born in a stable? It didn't seem possible.

Inside the cave a man knelt beside his young wife who lay upon a straw bed. The soft rock of the cave wall had been carved out to form a manger. That's where the feed for the animals was placed. There in that manger, on a bed of straw, was a newborn baby wrapped in strips of soft cloth. It was just as the angel had said.

As I looked at the baby, I was amazed at what we had seen and heard this night. Could this small baby, born in a stable, really be a king someday? Then I remembered the story of David, the shepherd who had become a king. This baby would someday become an even greater king than David. He would be the Savior of the world.

1. What were the shepherds doing when the angels appeared?

2. The angels' visit was a surprise with wonderful news for the shepherds. What are some good surprises you have had?

Journey to Jerusalem

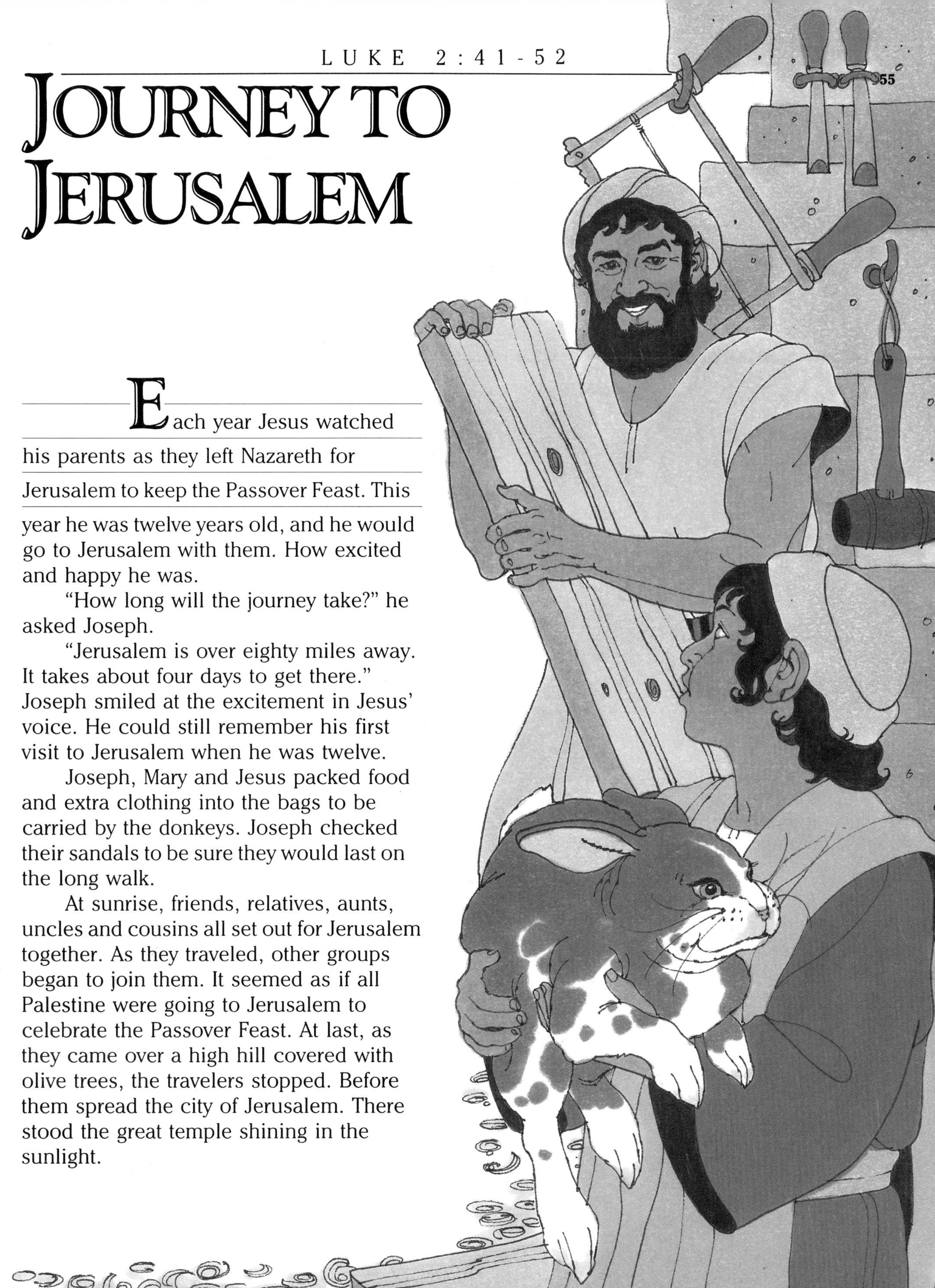

Each year Jesus watched his parents as they left Nazareth for Jerusalem to keep the Passover Feast. This year he was twelve years old, and he would go to Jerusalem with them. How excited and happy he was.

"How long will the journey take?" he asked Joseph.

"Jerusalem is over eighty miles away. It takes about four days to get there." Joseph smiled at the excitement in Jesus' voice. He could still remember his first visit to Jerusalem when he was twelve.

Joseph, Mary and Jesus packed food and extra clothing into the bags to be carried by the donkeys. Joseph checked their sandals to be sure they would last on the long walk.

At sunrise, friends, relatives, aunts, uncles and cousins all set out for Jerusalem together. As they traveled, other groups began to join them. It seemed as if all Palestine were going to Jerusalem to celebrate the Passover Feast. At last, as they came over a high hill covered with olive trees, the travelers stopped. Before them spread the city of Jerusalem. There stood the great temple shining in the sunlight.

They hurried into the city to find places to stay. Each family got ready for the Passover Feast. Meat was roasted, wild lettuce and other bitter herbs were gathered, and the flat bread was baked. When everything was ready, Joseph, Mary and their family gathered around the table. Joseph began the celebration with the Passover blessing. Then the feast was eaten. Now was the time for Jesus to ask the special questions.

Looking at Joseph, Jesus asked, "What is the meaning of this feast? What makes this night special?"

Joseph then told again the story of Israel's escape from Egypt.

When the feasts, sacrifices and celebrations were over, the family started on the long trip home.

"Have you seen Jesus?" Mary asked.

"He's probably with the other children," Joseph answered. "You know how excited they are and how they run ahead of the group."

But when they stopped for the night, Jesus was not there. Joseph and Mary searched everywhere, asking, "Have you seen Jesus?" But no one had seen him. He was lost.

Early the next morning they returned to Jerusalem. "Perhaps we will meet him on the way," said Joseph. Many travelers passed them, but none had seen a lost boy.

Mary and Joseph rested overnight in Jerusalem and began their search again the next morning. He was not where they had stayed during the feast. They were very worried and frightened. Jesus had been gone for three days. Where could he be?

"Let's go to the temple. Maybe someone has seen him there," they said.

As they entered the courtyard, they heard voices from one of the temple courts. There, surrounded by teachers, sat Jesus. First he listened. Then he asked questions. The teachers seemed amazed by how much he knew. They talked to him as if he were one of them.

"My son," Mary said, "why have you done this to us? We've been very worried. We've looked everywhere for you."

Jesus looked at his mother as if he did not understand. "Why have you been looking for me? Didn't you know that you would find me here in my Father's house?"

How thankful Joseph and Mary were that they had found Jesus safe. They were glad to have their family together again.

---

1. What special things happened when Jesus went to Jerusalem the first time?

2. Think about a special trip you and your family have taken together. What did you like best about it?

MARK 2:1-12

THE HOLE IN THE ROOF

"He's back! He's back!" My friends came running into my small room shouting the good news. "Jesus has come back to Capernaum."

"Where is he? Can you take me there?" I asked. I had been waiting for weeks. Jesus had healed many people, and I was sure he could heal me.

"Jesus is staying at Peter's house. But people from everywhere have come to hear him. The courtyard is full, and some are even standing in the street. I don't know if we can get you close enough to see him."

"Take me there anyway," I told my four friends. "He's the only one who can help. If you don't take me, I'll have to spend the rest of my life lying here on this mat, unable to move."

"We will find some way for you to see Jesus. I know he can heal you. He has healed others who couldn't walk."

Each of my friends picked up a corner of my mat and lifted me from the floor. It was the only way I could get around. They carried me through the streets. As we came near the house, I could hear the noise of the crowd. There were hundreds of people standing around! Even the street was full. Jesus was standing in a doorway under the cover of the courtyard, but there was no way to reach him.

"We'll never get through this crowd," said one of my friends.

"I've got an idea," said another. "There's a stairway at the side of the house. We'll carry you up the stairs to the roof."

"How will that help?" I asked.

"You'll see." With that, they picked up my mat and off we went. Around the crowd and up the stairs they carried me. Suddenly, they lifted me over the low wall around the edge of the flat roof and put me down above the porch. Then I heard the sounds of roof tiles being moved.

"What are you doing?" I asked.

"We're taking you to see Jesus."

As I turned my head, I couldn't believe my eyes. My friends were making a big hole in the roof. My heart was beating fast with excitement. Would I finally get to see Jesus? Would he heal me? I knew he could if only I could reach him.

I felt my mat being lifted. Each friend held a corner. They lay down on their stomachs and lowered the mat through the hole in the roof.

The sound of Jesus' voice stopped. A hush fell over the crowd as they watched me being lowered in front of them. Then I looked into his face. Would he be angry because I had stopped his teaching? No. There was only love and kindness in his smile.

He said, "My son, I have forgiven your sins. Stand up, pick up your bed and go home."

Immediately, my legs and arms felt stronger. I could move my body! I wanted to shout with joy. I hardly noticed the excitement of the people who watched me. Suddenly, they began to praise God and say, "We've never seen such an amazing thing before!"

Quickly, I picked up my mat and began praising God. I had seen Jesus. He had healed me with his mighty power, and I could walk again!

---

1. How did the man's friends help him see Jesus? What happened to him then?

2. Sometimes we need help to do things that are very important to us. What are some ways your friends and family have helped you do something that was important to you?

STORM AT SEA

Jesus and his followers had just come from Capernaum. There Jesus had been teaching and talking with people beside the Sea of Galilee. Great crowds had followed him from town to town. When he stopped, people pushed and shoved each other to get near him. Many sick people reached out to touch him, believing that just a touch would heal them.

"Jesus is tired," Peter said. "Let's see if we can get him to leave the crowds for a little while."

"You're right," said one of the other followers. "The crowds are getting bigger and bigger."

Jesus knew his followers' thoughts. He stood on the shore by the fishing boats watching the evening light on the water. The sea was quiet and peaceful. Leaving the crowds for a little while would be nice, and it would give him time to rest. Perhaps he could share his message of love with those who lived on the other side of the sea.

Pointing to a boat that belonged to one of the followers, he said, "Let's go to the other shore."

The followers were glad. The night air on the water would be restful after the hot day.

"We may have to row for a while," Peter said. "But when we get away from the shore, we will put up the sail and catch the evening breeze."

Though the boat was small, there was enough room for Jesus and his friends. Slowly, they began to move across the sea toward the shore ten miles away.

"Lord, why don't you lie down back here. This cushion is soft, and you can rest on it. We will be quiet," they said. Soon, they were resting, too.

Suddenly, everything began to change. A strong wind blew across the lake and began rocking the boat. Black clouds filled the sky, and rain came pouring down. Flashes of lightning danced in the sky. Roaring waves and thunder filled the night with noise.

"Get the sail down, or we will be blown over!" Peter shouted. Even as he spoke, the wind tore away the sail.

"Water is coming over the sides of the boat! Someone man the oars! We're sinking!" Everyone was yelling and shouting. "Call Jesus. We need his help!"

"Wake up, Lord. We're sinking. Save us before we all drown!" they cried in panic.

Jesus spoke calmly. "Where is your faith? You don't need to be so afraid." Then he stood and faced the storm. "Stop blowing!" he said to the wind. "Be quiet!" he commanded the waves.

No sooner had he spoken the words than the wind stopped. The sea became as smooth as glass. All was calm again.

The followers looked at each other in surprise and wonder. They knew Jesus was a teacher and a healer, but what was this?

"Who can this man be?" they asked each other. "When he speaks, even the sea and the wind obey him. He has the power of God!"

---

1. What happened while Jesus' friends were taking him across the Sea of Galilee in the boat?

2. Jesus calmed the storm so his friends wouldn't be afraid. What can you do when you are afraid? How do your friends and family help you?

MARK 6:30-44

A Big Picnic

"I see them! They're over in that old boat. They must be going to the other side of the lake," I said, pointing to Jesus and his followers.

"Let's follow them," my friend said, scrambling to his feet. "Maybe we'll get to see Jesus do another miracle. Come on. If we hurry, we can get there before they can row across the lake."

"Wait a minute," I told my friend. "I want to get something to eat. It's a long way over there, and there isn't any place to buy food."

I ran to my house. Picking up a basket, I put in five small loaves of flat barley bread and two salted fish left over from our lunch. I hurried to catch my friend. By the time I had reached the path that goes around the lake, many other people were there, too.

"Can you see what's happening?" I asked my friend.

"Jesus has stopped by the shore. Oh, look! He's talking to some of the sick people who have been carried here on mats. He's healing them! I wish we could get closer."

At last Jesus began to walk up the hill. As he sat down, everyone gathered around him. All afternoon he talked, telling how God loves us and how we should love each other. Even when the sun began to set, everyone stayed to listen to him.

Finally, one of Jesus' followers said to him, "Master, send the crowd away. They need to find food and a place to stay. There's nothing to eat on this side of the lake."

"They don't have to go away, Philip. You feed them," Jesus said.

"Feed them?" Philip looked surprised. "That would take all the money I could earn in eight months. Even that would buy only a small bit of food for each person."

Just then I noticed Andrew, one of Jesus' followers, walking through the crowd. As he came near, he asked me, "What's in your basket?"

"Just five small loaves of bread and two fish," I answered.

"Come with me," he said, taking me by the hand. As we came to Jesus, Andrew said, "This boy has five barley loaves and two fish, but they won't go very far in feeding all these people."

"Give them to me," Jesus said.

Taking the loaves and fish, he said to the people, "Get together in groups of fifty, and sit down." What was he going to do with my small basket of food? There were five thousand men there, not counting the women and children.

First, Jesus looked up to heaven and gave thanks. Next, he broke the loaves into pieces and gave them to his followers. As they began passing out the bread, Jesus broke the fish into pieces, and his friends passed them out also. Something strange was happening! There was enough bread and fish for everyone! In fact, there was more than we could eat. When everyone was finished, Jesus' followers gathered twelve full baskets of leftovers!

Suddenly, I knew I had just seen a miracle. Jesus had fed over five thousand people with my five loaves and two fish. The people were amazed. They said, "Truly, this is the Savior who has come into the world." And I knew that they were right.

---

1. What did the boy have that Jesus used to make a miracle happen?

2. Jesus showed his love and care when he fed the hungry people. Tell about a time you shared food with someone.

MATTHEW 14:22-36

A WALK ON THE WATER

What an amazing day! Jesus had fed five thousand people with only five small loaves of bread and two fish. But now he was tired and wanted to be alone for a while.

"Get into the boat and go to the other side of the lake," he said to us, his followers. "I will send all these people back to their homes. Then I'm going up into the hills to pray. I will meet you at Bethsaida on the other side of the lake."

Jesus sometimes liked to pray alone; so we did as he asked. As we began to row away from the shore, the last rays of the setting sun made the water look like sparkling silver and gold. The hills on the other side of the lake made long shadows in the water. The night grew quiet, and the sky darkened. Here and there a star twinkled, peeking out between the clouds. A breeze began to rock the small boat. But soon the breeze turned into a strong wind.

"Row harder. We're being pushed back to the other side," Peter shouted.

"We aren't moving very much. How far have we come?" someone asked.

"About three and a half miles. We're only about halfway across," another answered.

The wind blew harder and harder, slamming the waves against the boat. We began to worry. We had been rowing for hours, but the shore seemed just as far away as before.

"Look!" someone shouted. "What's that?"

"Something is coming across the water!"

"It's a ghost!" someone cried. We were terrified.

"Don't be frightened. It is I," said a familiar voice. It was Jesus!

We couldn't believe what we were seeing. Jesus was walking on the stormy lake as if it were a path through a quiet garden.

"Lord, if it is really you, tell me to come out to meet you," shouted Peter. We all stared at him with disbelief.

"Come then," said Jesus.

Carefully Peter crawled out of the boat onto the stormy water of the lake. He took one step, then another and another. The wind howled and pushed against the water, making waves that washed about Peter's feet. Everything was fine until Peter noticed what was happening. The wind was whipping the water, and he was walking on it!

Suddenly he was afraid. At that moment he began to sink into the darkness of the stormy sea.

"Oh, Jesus, save me!" Peter cried as he felt the cold water begin to swallow him.

Quickly Jesus reached out his hand and pulled Peter up from the waves.

"What a little bit of faith you have!" Jesus said. "Why did you start to think you couldn't do it?"

Peter had no answer. He and Jesus just climbed back into the boat. Suddenly, the wind stopped. If we had had any doubts about this man, they were gone now. No one else could do such wonderful things. Jesus is the Son of God!

---

1. What did Jesus do to help his friends in the boat?

2. When Peter sank into the sea, he called out to Jesus for help. Tell about a time you asked someone for help.

LUKE 10:25-37

THE ROBBERS AND THE NEIGHBOR

Jesus told a story about a man who was going from Jerusalem to Jericho. The road turned and twisted as it went down into the valley of the Jordan River.

The man was traveling alone on the hot, dusty road. As he passed some large rocks, robbers jumped out and grabbed him.

"Give us your money and all your belongings," the robbers demanded.

The man was so scared. He quickly gave them his money bag and the few things he had with him.

"Take off your clothes and give them to us too," one of the robbers said.

After taking everything he had, the robbers beat the man too. They left him lying in the road, half dead.

After a long time a priest came along. "At last there is someone to help me," the man thought. "A priest knows God's law. He knows God expects everyone to help people who are in trouble. I'm a Jew as he is. Surely the priest will help me."

When the priest came near, he saw the helpless man lying there. But the priest didn't stop to help. He crossed to the other side of the road! He went past as if he didn't care at all about the poor man.

A little while later a Levite came walking down the road. The Levites were the men who served God in the temple. "Surely a Levite will stop and help me," the man thought.

But the Levite paid no attention to the injured man lying in the dirt. He was just like the priest. He also hurried by on the other side of the road.

The sun was beating down on the injured man, and he was very thirsty. He was about to give up hope, when he saw someone else coming. It was a stranger,

someone from another part of the country. It was a Samaritan. Jews and Samaritans had been enemies for years. They wouldn't even talk to each other. "A Samaritan would never stop to help me," he thought.

But the Samaritan did stop. Getting off his donkey he stooped down and looked at the man's wounds. From a bundle in his pack, he took medicines and bandages. Gently he doctored the man's wounds. Then he brought his donkey near and carefully lifted the injured man onto the donkey's back. The Samaritan walked along beside as they went down the road to an inn where they could spend the night.

The Samaritan took care of the man until morning. When it was time for the Samaritan to leave, he called to the innkeeper. He said, "Take care of this fellow. Here is money for you. If this isn't enough, I'll pay you for everything extra you spend when I come by here again."

When Jesus finished telling this story, he turned to a young man and asked, "Which of these three men acted like a neighbor?"

"The one who was kind and helpful," he answered.

"Go your way," Jesus said, "and be a good neighbor, too."

---

1. How did the Samaritan show he was a good neighbor?

2. Can you think of a time when you helped someone who was in trouble?

LUKE 15:11-31

ROUND TRIP

As Jesus walked along on the way to Jerusalem, he told this story to the people traveling with him.

Once there was a father who had two sons. The younger son was not happy living at home and helping run the farm. One day he said, "Father, give me the part of the family money that will someday be mine."

So the father divided everything he had and gave part to the younger son and part to the older. Soon afterward the young son packed his things and the money his father had given him. He decided to go to a land far away where he could do as he pleased. Leaving his older brother at home with his father, the boy set out.

After many days he arrived in the new country. For a while he enjoyed life with his new friends. He gave them gifts and big parties. He noticed how quickly he was using up his money, but he did not want to disappoint anyone.

Finally, all his money was gone. Then his new friends quickly forgot him. They hadn't cared about him at all; they had just liked his money. Now he needed to work to earn his living, but there were no jobs to be found. His once fine clothes became worn and old, and he didn't have any money to buy more. Soon he began to be hungry because he had no money for food either.

At last he found a job taking care of pigs. It was the worst job he could think of, but it was the only one he could find. So he took it. No one offered him anything to eat. He was so hungry even the pigs' food looked good to him.

The boy thought about what he had done. How foolish he had been to waste all his money on parties and having a good time. How badly he had treated his family. He missed them so much. He wished he had not left the farm. Even the poorest of his father's hired workers had good food to eat. Yet, here he was, almost starving.

"I know what I'll do," he said. "I'll go back home. I've been wrong. I'll tell my father I'm not good enough to be his son. I'll ask him to let me work as one of his hired men."

So the boy set out on the long journey. As he walked along, he began to wonder, "Will my father let me come home again? How will he treat me?"

The father had missed his younger son very much. He would often look down the road, hoping that someday the boy would return. One afternoon as the father was looking in the distance, he saw someone coming down the road. There was something familiar about that walk. It was his son! The father ran out to meet him and hugged and kissed him. How happy he was to have his son home again.

"Father," the boy said, "I have done wrong against you and against God. I'm not good enough to be your son anymore."

"Servants!" the father called. "Bring the best clothes and shoes for my son. Put a ring on his finger. We're going to have a celebration. Prepare a great feast. My son was gone, but now he is back with me again."

Because he loved his son very much, the father had forgiven all the wrong his son had done. God's love is like that, too.

---

1. How do you know the boy's father loved him and forgave him for what he had done?

2. Tell about a time someone forgave you.

JOHN 11:1-44

LAZARUS LIVES!

"Wake up! Wake up!"

"I'm awake, Mother. What's wrong?"

"I've just come from Mary and Martha's house. I'm afraid their brother Lazarus is dying. You must carry a message to their friend Jesus. Go tell him about Lazarus. And hurry! Lazarus may not live through another night."

I knew the way to the place where Jesus was, but I had never gone that far alone. Still, I'd try anything to help Lazarus.

When I set out, the morning was chilly, but the day grew warmer as I walked. I crossed the Jordan and was thankful that the river was not in flood. At noon I ate flat bread and cheese from my pack. Finally, at sunset, I found Jesus and his friends.

"Teacher, come quickly. Your friend Lazarus is ill. He'll die unless you come heal him."

"No, Lazarus will not die now," Jesus said. "This illness will show how great God is."

I had hurried all day to bring this urgent message, but Jesus didn't seem worried. How could Lazarus' illness be good? I didn't say anything, but I was upset. Surely we would go tomorrow. But we didn't leave the next day...or the next day either. Why couldn't I make him understand? Lazarus would die if Jesus didn't come soon.

Finally, on the third day Jesus said to his friends, "We must go back to Judea."

His followers were surprised. "The people there just tried to kill you! Now you want to go back?"

"Yes, because Lazarus is dead," Jesus answered sadly.

So we set out early in the morning. The trip seemed endless, but by late evening we could see Bethany in the distance. Sounds of people crying came from the house of Mary, Martha and Lazarus. Before we reached it, Martha came to meet us. She looked tired, and her eyes were red from crying.

"Oh, Lord," she sobbed. "Lazarus is dead. We buried him four days ago. If only you had been here, he wouldn't have died."

"Your brother will live again, Martha," Jesus answered her.

When Mary, her sister, heard that Jesus had come, she came and fell at his feet. "Oh, Lord, if you had been here, Lazarus wouldn't have died," she sobbed.

I looked at Jesus. Tears had filled his eyes and were running down his face. How much he must have loved Lazarus.

"Where have you put his body?" he asked.

They led Jesus into a small garden. A cave had been dug into a hillside, and a rounded stone covered the opening.

Then Jesus said, "Move the stone away from the opening."

"But Lord," Martha objected, "he's been dead for four days."

"Remember," Jesus answered, "if you believe, you will see how great God is."

Jesus' followers rolled back the stone. Jesus looked up to God and prayed. Then he called in a loud voice, "Lazarus, come out!"

Jesus was talking to a dead man! I held my breath, watching the opening of the cave. Something was moving inside! Suddenly, a person was standing in the mouth of the tomb. His hands, feet, body and even his face were wrapped in white cloths. Could it really be Lazarus?

Jesus spoke again. "Take off his burial cloths, and let him go."

There stood Lazarus before us, alive and well! A miracle! At last it was clear. Jesus has power over life and death. He is the Son of God!

---

1. Even though Jesus had the power to bring Lazarus back to life, he still cried at his death. Why?

---

2. How can we show people who are sick that we love them?

LUKE 19:1-10

A SURPRISE VISIT

Zacchaeus looked out the second story window of his beautiful house. In the street beyond the courtyard a large group of people were talking excitedly.

"What's going on?" Zacchaeus shouted to them.

The people stopped, looked up at Zacchaeus and turned their backs to him as if he were not even there. It didn't surprise him. He was the chief tax collector for Jericho, and everybody hated the tax collectors. They often cheated people and charged them more than they really owed. The job had made Zacchaeus very rich. He liked the money, but it would be nice to have some friends.

"Oh well," he said to himself, "if I want to know why everyone is so excited, I'll just have to find out for myself." With that he went downstairs and out into the crowded street. "What's going on?" he asked a beggar, dropping a coin into his bowl.

"Jesus, the teacher and healer, is coming through Jericho. He just cured the blind man who begged outside the city gates. I saw the man myself, and now he can see as well as you can."

Zacchaeus had heard of Jesus and his teachings. People said that he had even

brought a man back to life in nearby Bethany.

"I want to see this teacher," Zacchaeus thought. But the street was even more crowded than before. "I wish I were not so short," Zacchaeus muttered to himself. "I can't see anything but people's backs." He tried to push through the people to reach the edge of the tree-lined street.

"Watch what you're doing, Zacchaeus," said an unfriendly man as he pushed Zacchaeus even further back into the crowd.

Zacchaeus was determined to see Jesus, but no matter how much he pushed and shoved he couldn't get through. And no matter how hard he tried, he couldn't see over the people in front of him.

Then he had an idea. Hurrying through the crowd, he went down the street and climbed into a sycamore tree beside it. From the noise of the crowd he knew Jesus was getting near. At last he found just the branch he wanted. Crawling out onto it, he pushed aside the big leaves to watch.

People were shouting questions to Jesus. Mothers held up their babies so he could see them. The sick and crippled cried out for him to heal them. At last Jesus was almost under the tree. Zacchaeus could see his kind face. "He would never

talk to me, a tax collector," Zacchaeus thought.

Just then Jesus stopped and looked up into the tree where Zacchaeus was sitting. "Zacchaeus, come down out of that tree. Today I'm going to visit in your house."

"You're most welcome in my home!" Zacchaeus cried with joy. He couldn't believe it! Jesus had called him by name. And he was coming to his home! Climbing down quickly out of the tree, he took Jesus by the hand and led him to his house.

When the crowd saw this, they began to complain. "He's gone to the house of a sinner. What a terrible person for him to visit!"

But inside the house something wonderful was happening. As Zacchaeus listened to Jesus, he decided to change the way he lived. He said,"Lord, today I'm going to give half of everything I own to the poor. If I've taken anything unfairly, I'll give back four times as much as I took."

Zacchaeus felt warm and wonderful. His life had changed. Even though he was a small man, he would do big things for Jesus. Suddenly, he felt nine feet tall!

---

1. What problems did Zacchaeus have when he tried to see Jesus? How did he solve them?

2. Zacchaeus gave his money to the poor because he was so full of Jesus' love. What have you given to someone just because you loved them?

SERVANT AND MASTER

At last it was time. We had waited all day for this special dinner. Tonight we would celebrate the Passover meal. Each year the Jewish people eat this special meal to remind them of how God helped the people of Israel to escape from Egyptian slavery.

Just before midnight Jesus and all of us who are his followers met together in an upstairs room. Everything was ready. There were thirteen cushions around the table where we would sit. Small olive oil lamps gave a yellow light to the room. Roast lamb, bitter herbs, flat bread and the Passover wine were on the table.

We gathered around the table. On one side sat John, Jesus and Judas. The other followers sat down along the sides and at one end. I was at the end across from John. Jesus offered a prayer of blessing and thanksgiving, and the feast began.

Suddenly, Jesus got up from the table and took off the white outer coat he was wearing. He tucked a drying towel around his waist and poured water into a bowl. Was he going to wash his hands? No, he brought the bowl to the table. Then he knelt in front of me. What was he doing? Jesus was my teacher, my Lord, God's own son, but he was acting like a house servant. It was a servant's job to meet a guest at the door, take off his sandals and wash his dusty, dirty feet after a long walk.

"Are you planning to wash my feet?" I asked.

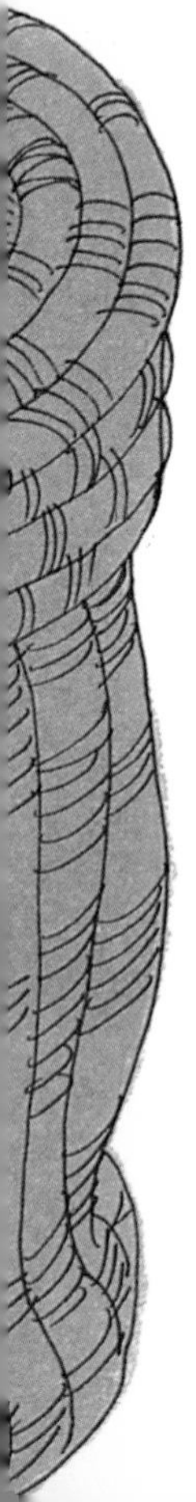

"You may not understand what I am doing now, but someday you will," Jesus answered.

"I won't let you wash my feet," I told him.

"Peter," he said, "unless you let me do this, you can't be my helper."

I was confused. I didn't understand, but I knew I wanted to help Jesus. So I said, "Then, please Lord, don't just wash my feet. Wash my head and hands, too."

So Jesus washed my feet. Like a servant he washed the feet of each person at the table. As we watched, we wondered, "Why is the Son of God doing this for us? Why is he acting like a servant? After all, he is the Lord, our master."

When Jesus finished, he put on his white coat again and returned to the table. “Do you understand what I just did?” he asked. When no one answered, he said, “You call me your Lord and teacher, and that is right. If I, your Lord and teacher, have been a helper to you, you should be willing to help each other also. This is an example of how you should act. You’re not better than your teacher, just as a servant isn’t better than his master. If you will be a servant and helper to other people, you will be blessed.”

I remembered the times we had quarreled about who was most important to Jesus. He had told us that the most important people were not the ones who acted important. Jesus said the most important people were the ones who served and helped others.

---

1. How did Jesus show his friends they should serve others?

---

2. What can you do to serve your mother, father, friends or teachers?

SOMEONE'S AT THE DOOR

It was a sad, frightening time for the Christians in Jerusalem. King Herod was punishing Christians for believing in Jesus. Many people had been arrested and put in jail. And now, Peter had been arrested too.

"Send sixteen soldiers to guard this man," Herod said. "He's a leader of the Christians. Make sure he doesn't escape. I'll deal with him later."

So Peter was taken deep into the prison. Each of his wrists was chained to a soldier, one on one side and one on the other. Outside his cell and in front of the prison gate many other soldiers stood guard.

Late that night Peter lay sleeping with his arms still chained to the soldiers. The dark prison was quiet. The only sounds were the clinking of chains and the soft, sad voices of the other prisoners.

Suddenly, someone else was in the cell! A bright light broke through the darkness. God had sent an angel to Peter!

"Quick," the angel said, touching Peter's side to wake him. "Get up." As the angel spoke, the heavy chains fell off Peter's wrists, and his hands were free. "Put on your sandals, and get into your clothes," said the angel. "Take your coat and come with me."

"Surely I must be dreaming or having a vision. This can't really be happening," Peter thought as he put on his clothes and followed the angel out of his cell.

Soon they came to the guard post of the inner prison. But no one moved or even seemed to notice as Peter and the angel walked by! Ahead was the second group of soldiers, who guarded the prison entrance. Again Peter and the angel walked right past them. Then they came to the great locked gates of the prison. As the angel came near the gates, they swung open by themselves! Peter was free!

Peter and the angel walked outside and down the street. Then, as suddenly as he had come, the angel disappeared, leaving Peter alone in the darkness.

"It's true!" Peter said to himself. "An angel of the Lord has helped me escape from Herod's prison." Peter hurried through the town until he reached Mary's house. Many of his friends had come there to pray. They had heard that Peter was in prison, and they had been praying to God to help him.

Peter knocked on the outside door.

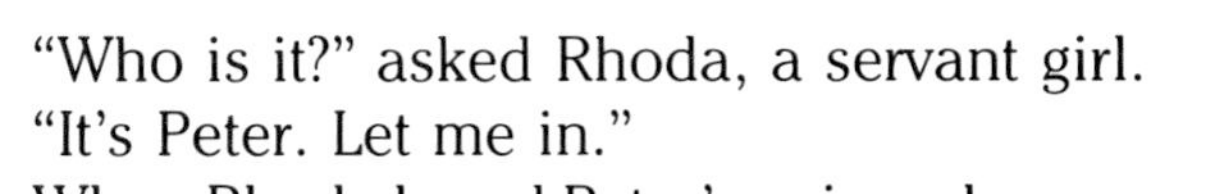

"Who is it?" asked Rhoda, a servant girl.

"It's Peter. Let me in."

When Rhoda heard Peter's voice, she was so excited she forgot to unlock the door. Leaving him standing outside, she ran back into the house shouting, "Peter is at the door! It's Peter!"

"You've lost your mind," they told her. "Peter is in prison."

"But it's true. Peter is at the door," she said. But they still didn't believe her.

Peter knocked and knocked. Finally they opened the door. It really was Peter! Everyone began talking and asking questions at once.

Peter waved his hand to quiet them. When they heard the wonderful thing that had happened, they knew God had rescued Peter from prison. God had answered their prayers.

---

1. What did the Christians in Jerusalem do for Peter when he was in prison?

2. How can we help our friends when they are sad?

ACTS 16:22-40

EARTHQUAKE IN PHILIPPI

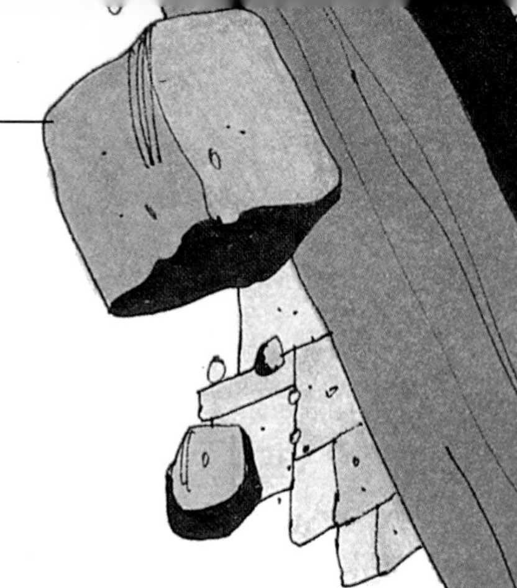

"Strip them and beat them. Then put them in prison," said the mayor, pointing to us. He had believed the lies the mob had told him about us. Paul and I had been in Philippi for several weeks telling people about the love of Jesus. We had done nothing wrong, but now we were prisoners!

The jailer did as he had been told. After the beating, he locked us in cells deep inside the prison. Our feet were locked between heavy wooden boards called stocks, and our hands and necks were chained to the wall. We couldn't sit or stand, and our backs ached from the terrible beating.

"Silas." I was glad to hear Paul's voice and know he was alive.

"I'm here, Paul."

"Let's pray and sing praises to God."

That's what I love about Paul. No matter how terrible things may seem, he can always find a reason to be thankful. He's always sure that whatever happens, God will make it turn out for the best. Yes, we should sing and praise God, I thought. We're alive! We've told many people about Jesus. God will take care of us.

So Paul and I prayed and sang. Although it was almost midnight, the other prisoners sat listening. Perhaps songs of praise and thanksgiving coming from a prison cell sounded strange to them. But the more we sang, the better I felt.

Suddenly, the walls and floor of the prison began to tremble and shake. The stones rumbled, and the iron chains and bars rattled. An earthquake was rolling through the prison! Would the walls tumble in? Would we be trapped? Just then our chains popped loose, and the prison doors swung open! A miracle had happened! God had set us free.

The jailer came running to our cell. When he saw all the doors open, he was sure his prisoners had escaped. He knew a jailer would be killed if he let his prisoners escape. He drew his sword, planning to kill himself.

"Don't do that!" Paul shouted. "No one has escaped. We're all still here."

The jailer couldn't believe what he had heard. He called for lights to be brought. When he could see, he ran into our cell and fell to his knees before us. Trembling, he led us out of the cell.

This fellow must have heard that we served God and Jesus. He saw that God had helped us. So he turned to us and said, "What can I do to be saved?"

"You must believe in the Lord Jesus," Paul and I told him. "You and everyone in your house can be saved if you believe in him."

The jailer took us away from the awful prison. With his own hands he washed and cleaned the cuts and bruises on our backs. How sorry he was for what he had done. Paul and I told the jailer and his family the story of Jesus and how to obey him. When they heard these things, the jailer and all his family were baptized.

We went to the jailer's house. He gave us food and treated us like honored guests. How quickly God's word changes people. Last night this man had beaten us and locked us up like criminals. Today, he cared for our wounds and fed us like friends. He and his family now believed in God. They were so happy to know that God loved them.

Paul was right. God can make anything turn out for the best.

---

1. How did the jailer show he was sorry for the way he had treated Paul and Silas?

2. Paul and Silas helped each other by praying and singing to God. When do you and your family sing and pray together?

ESCAPE FROM JERUSALEM

"Mother, Mother, they've arrested Uncle Paul! He was talking to the high council when suddenly everyone began to shout and argue. Then soldiers came and pushed everyone away. They took Uncle Paul away, but he didn't do anything wrong."

"I know," Mother answered. "Paul was just telling people about Jesus, but some people don't want to hear about Jesus."

"Why does he keep preaching to them then?" I asked.

"Your uncle loves Jesus very much, and he wants others to know about Jesus' love. Uncle Paul is a Christian. He has promised to serve Jesus no matter what happens."

“Even if they put him in prison and hurt him?” I asked.

“Yes, even if they do worse things than that,” she answered. “Perhaps if you went down to the soldiers’ barracks you could ask one of the guards what has happened.”

As I hurried through the streets, I saw a large group of men whispering together. They were the ones who had been yelling at my uncle. They were up to something. Keeping out of sight, I crept closer to hear what they were saying.

“We must kill Paul, or he will keep on preaching about Jesus. Let’s make a promise that we will not eat or drink anything until we have killed him! Here’s how we’ll do it. We’ll get the high council to ask the commander to bring Paul to the temple. When they come by here, we will attack and kill him.” And all the men agreed!

I had to do something—quick. I ran to the great stone barracks as fast as my legs would carry me. Finding my uncle, I yelled out, “Uncle Paul! Some men are planning to kill you!”

“Guard!” my uncle said. “Take this young man to see your commander. He has something he must tell him.”

The soldier led me to the commander. “This fellow has something to tell you,” the soldier said as he saluted.

The commander led me to one side of the room. “What do you have to say?” he asked.

Quickly I told him the plan, and he believed me. Looking very serious, he said, “Don’t tell anyone else what you have told me.”

Then he called two of his officers and began giving orders. “Get two hundred soldiers, seventy horsemen and two hundred spearmen ready. We will leave at nine o’clock for Caesarea. I want Paul taken to Governor Felix in safety.”

Exactly on time the gates of the fortress opened, and the soldiers marched out with my Uncle Paul in the middle of them. He would be safe now. Soon he would be in Caesarea. As I waved good-by, I thought about how the Lord had taken care of him. The Lord would find a way for Paul to tell many more people about the love of Jesus.

1. Why do you think Paul kept preaching to people about Jesus, even when they were unkind to him?

2. How did Paul's nephew show his courage and bravery in the story? When are some times we need to show courage and bravery?

ACTS 27

SHIPWRECKED

"It's a Northeaster!" shouted a sailor.

Paul and I were caught in the worst kind of storm. We were sailing to Rome where Paul would stand trial before Caesar. Our trip had been a difficult one. The ship had been tossed around by high winds, and there had already been one terrible storm. Now we were caught in another one!

Quickly the sailors tied the smaller boats to the deck. On and on the winds drove us. The wooden planks began to pull apart, and the sailors had to tie great ropes around the whole ship to hold it together.

The waves were higher than the ship! The captain ordered all boxes and bundles thrown overboard so we wouldn't sink. Everyone was sure we would be swallowed up by the angry sea.

Paul called everyone to him. "If you had listened to me, none of this would have happened. I warned you not to set sail yet. But be brave. The Lord I serve sent an angel to me last night. He told me not to be afraid because I will reach Rome to stand trial before Caesar. He also said that although the ship will sink, all your lives will be saved. Now be brave and believe what God has said. It will turn out just that way. The ship will run aground on an island."

The sailors felt much better after what Paul said, but the storm continued to toss us about. On the fourteenth day, the wind began blowing us into shallow water. Several of the sailors became afraid that the ship would be dashed against the rocks. They pretended they were lowering an anchor in the water. But, instead, they were lowering the lifeboat. They were going to escape and leave us behind! But Paul warned them that they had to stay with the ship or they would drown. So the soldiers cut the ropes, and the lifeboat was swept away.

Before dawn the next day, Paul called

the men to him again. "You've been very worried and have gone without food for days. Now eat something. No one is going to be hurt." Then Paul gave thanks for the bread we had, and all of the men ate and felt better.

When daylight came, we could see an island ahead. If we could just get there, we would be safe. The captain ordered us to throw overboard everything that was left. He cut loose the heavy anchors and headed the ship for the shore.

Suddenly, the bow of the ship hit a sandbar and stuck fast. Behind us, the raging waves began tearing the ship to pieces.

"Kill the prisoners so they won't escape," shouted the soldiers.

"No! Leave them alone," ordered Julius, the commander. "The ship is breaking up. Swim ashore if you can. If you can't, jump in the water and grab some of the floating wood or a piece of the ship."

Soldiers and prisoners alike jumped into the sea and began swimming for the shore. When everyone reached land, Julius counted us. All two hundred seventy-six of us were safe, just as Paul had said. The Lord had saved us just as he said he would. God always keeps his promises.

---

1. How did Paul know the ship would sink but the men would be saved?

---

2. Tell about a promise you made and how you kept it.